We can do no great things –
only small things with great love.

Mother Teresa (1910–1997)

My Thoughts ^{with} *Love*

A Grandparent's Keepsake Journal

ANNE GEDDES

My Thoughts with *Love*

from

Date

ife itself is the most wonderful fairy tale.

Hans Christian Andersen (1805–1875)

Date

Date

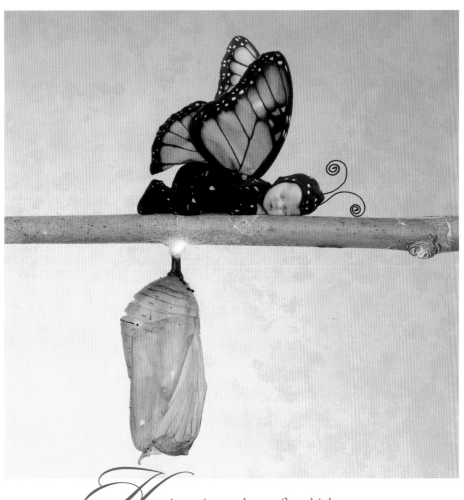

*Happiness is as a butterfly which,
when pursued, is always beyond our grasp,
but which, if you will sit down quietly,
may alight upon you.*

Nathaniel Hawthorne (1804–1864)

Date

Date

Babies are such a nice way to start people.

Don Herold (1889–1966)

Date

Date

Date

*D*o you believe in fairies?
… If you believe, clap your hands!

J. M. Barrie (1860–1937)

Date

Date

Date

*W*hat's in a name?
That which we call a rose
By any other name would smell as sweet.

William Shakespeare (1564–1616)

Date

Date

Angels can fly because they take themselves lightly.

G. K. Chesterton (1874–1936)

Date

Date

Date

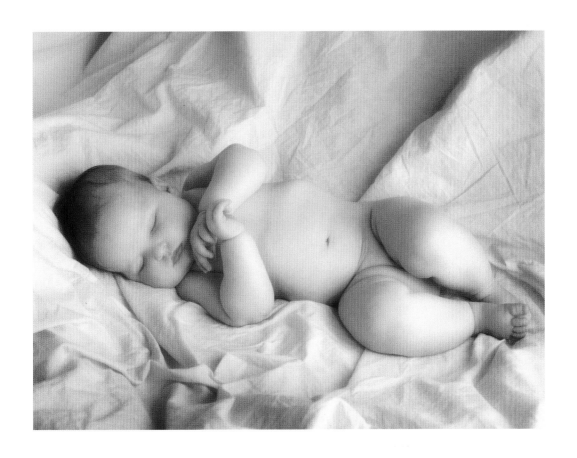

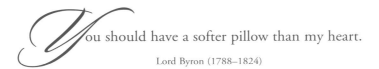ou should have a softer pillow than my heart.

Lord Byron (1788–1824)

Date

Date ....

Date

Oh! little lock of golden hue,
In gently waving ringlet curl'd,
By the dear head on which you grew,
I would not lose you for a world.

Lord Byron (1788–1824)

Date

Date

*L*ittle children are the most lovely flowers
this side of Eden.

Rev. Dr. Davies

Date

Date

Date

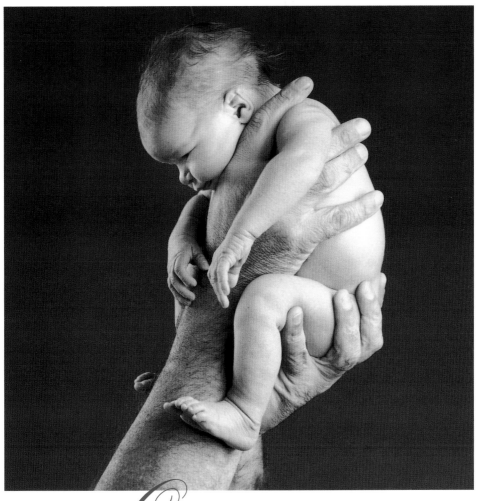

𝒪 wonderful, wonderful,
and most wonderful wonderful!
and yet again wonderful.

William Shakespeare (1564–1616)

Date

Date

Date

Those who bring sunshine
to the lives of others
cannot keep it from themselves.

J. M. Barrie (1860–1937)

Date

Date

Date ....

$\mathscr{T}$here are two ways to live your life.
One is as though nothing is a miracle.
The other is as though everything is a miracle.

Albert Einstein (1879–1955)

Date

Date

Date

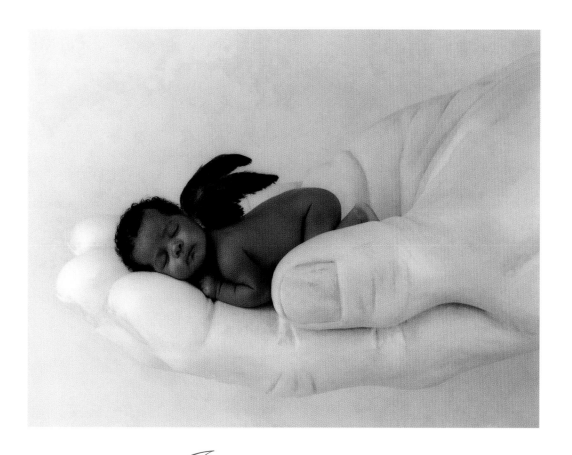

*I*t lay upon its mother's breast, a thing
Bright as a dewdrop when it first descends
Or as the plumage of an angel's wing,
Where every tint of rainbow beauty blends.

Amelia Welby (1821–1852)

Date

Date

Date

*T*he fragrance always stays in the hand
that gives the rose.

Hada Bejar

Date

Date

There are only two lasting bequests we can hope to give our children.
One of these is roots; the other, wings.

Cecilia Lasbury

Date

Date

The very pink of perfection.

Oliver Goldsmith (1728–1774)

ANNE GEDDES ™

ISBN 0-7683-2084-4

© Anne Geddes 1999

Published in 1999 by Photogenique Publishers
(a division of Hodder Moa Beckett)
Studio 3.16, Axis Building, 1 Cleveland Road, Parnell
Auckland, New Zealand

First USA edition published in 1999 by Cedco Publishing Company,
100 Pelican Way, San Rafael, CA 94901

Designed by Lucy Richardson
Produced by Kel Geddes
Color separations by MH Group

Printed by Midas Printing Limited, Hong Kong

Please write to us for a FREE FULL COLOR catalogue of our
fine Anne Geddes calendars and books, Cedco Publishing Company,
100 Pelican Way, San Rafael, CA 94901
or visit our website: www.cedco.com
10 9 8 7 6 5 4 3 2 1